How to Survive a Disaster

Emergency Preparedness for You and Your Family

Judith Turnbridge

First Printing, 2013

Printed in the United States of America

Table of Contents

Where's a Superhero When You Need One?

You only have to switch on the TV or listen to the radio for a few moments to realize our world is a pretty dangerous place to live. Droughts, floods, wildfires, earthquakes, and hurricanes are just a few of the bewildering ways Mother Nature has tried to dispose of us. All too often, humans seem hell bent on adding to this list through misadventure, acts of war, and terrorism.

As our society grows, it becomes ever more dependent on complex systems of governance and infrastructure for its survival. Any of these can fail and lead to a disaster; a terrorist attack, the breaching of a levee, an explosion at a chemical plant, or radiation leak from a nuclear power station. Each of these disasters can lead to the loss of thousands of lives. In the aftermath of such tragedies, many more may encounter serious breakdowns in vital services or a lack of supplies that could last for days, weeks, or even months. Moreover, it is not only the "major" incidents that can lead to catastrophe.

One famous example took place on a hot, steamy, July evening back in 1977. A lightning strike tripped a couple of twenty dollar circuit breakers at an electrical substation. Because of shoddy maintenance, they failed to trip back on again. This set off a chain of events that lead to the most notorious blackout in New York's history. Over 3,700 people were arrested after an orgy of violence, arson, and looting that lasted throughout that night. Much of the city was without power for 23 hours.

However, many of us believe that such things couldn't happen or that the emergency service providers will take care of everything until life can return to normal again.

Unfortunately, recent trends and events suggest otherwise. A quick examination of FEMA's poor response to Hurricane Katrina should certainly challenge anyone's faith.

To further hamper their effectiveness, many of these emergency services have suffered savage cutbacks following the global economic downturn.

If that wasn't enough, our planet's changing climate is going to make things even tougher for these organizations (and for us) by raising the chances that these disasters will occur in the first place.

The vast majority of scientists believe that as the Earth gets warmer, its weather will become ever more unpredictable and extreme. This inevitably will lead to a steady increase in the number and severity of natural catastrophes, both in the U.S. and the rest of the world.

Perhaps it is not surprising that many Americans, concerned by climate change and shaken by the recent performances of their emergency services, are relying on themselves to cope with disaster. That is where this book can help out.

This book is intended to provide practical tips on preparing for and surviving catastrophic events, both natural and manmade.

It is not intended for radical survivalists or anyone who believes that society is about to collapse around their ears; it is for the ordinary citizen who simply desires to protect themselves and their loved ones during times of crisis.

However, please be aware that I do not claim this book to be the definitive manual on dealing with disaster. It is merely a guide to some of the essential techniques that can be used to manage these potentially, life-threatening situations.

I've written this book in such a way that it can either be studied from cover to cover, or referred to at points relevant to your situation, although you should find many useful tips buried throughout.

Like many things in life, the more you prepare, the greater your chances of success. In this case, the stakes couldn't be higher since success here means survival. So, let us now turn to the next chapter and discover how to begin our preparations for disaster.

How to Prepare for an Emergency

Before we can do *anything* productive, we need a coherent plan in order to help us deal with a catastrophe.

The Disaster Plan

There are two parts to a disaster plan:

1. The evacuation plan

2. The shelter-in-place plan

You will need to draft both parts because you might have to swap between them as a crisis unfolds.

The reason for this is because events in a disaster can change in an instant and present you with a fresh set of challenges. For example, you may have intended to tough out a tornado, by staying inside your home and putting the shelter-in-place plan into use, only to find that your local levee is about to break and you need to relocate in a hurry. Now you will need to swing your evacuation plan into action.

For either of these to work, you'll need full cooperation from the members of your household. Therefore, you should gather your family and anyone else who is living with you to discuss the following points:

– How to prepare and respond to the emergencies that are most likely to happen where you live, learn, work, and play.

– Identify responsibilities for each member of your household. Plan how to work together as a team.

– If a family member is in the military, discuss the consequences for you if they were deployed for the relief effort.

– Make sure that preferably at least one member of your household is proficient in first aid, CPR, and even the use an automated external defibrillator (AED).

This last point is vital. Emergency services will almost certainly be in disarray in the immediate aftermath of a catastrophe, so it is very probable you will need to deal with any initial medical crises without their help. (Be sure to contact your local Red Cross about training courses.)

However, before we can do any type of planning, we need to figure out exactly what to plan for. We can do this by drafting a disasters list.

The Disasters List

The point of this exercise is to help organize your thoughts and clarify which crises to prepare for and which to ignore. It is crucial not to skip this step if you what to prepare effectively!

The first thing to do is grab a big sheet of paper and a pencil (or create an electronic spreadsheet if you prefer) and **list what types of disasters are possible in your area**. After all, there is little point in piling sandbags against your front door to protect against flooding if you live in the middle of the Nevada desert!

Be aware that there are many "scopes" to a disaster. Some of these can occur in the home, like a house fire or medical emergency. The dangers they present are often pretty obvious and straightforward to prepare for and deal with (such as ensuring your house is equipped with smoke alarms and fire blankets or that someone is proficient in first aid). There are some crises, however, like earthquakes or floods, which are very challenging because they can affect your entire community.

Next, **consider how frequently these crises may occur**. As a (very) rough rule of thumb, **focus only on the events that could happen within the next five years**. Cross out any on your list that cannot occur within this time period. (Remember, it is impossible to plan for every eventuality so it is pointless trying to do so.)

Next, prioritize your list by the likelihood of each event taking place and the dangers they would present to yourself and your loved ones if they were to happen.

How you approach this is step is up to you, but one method is to draw up a pair of columns next to your crisis list and give each one an appropriate heading (i.e. 'Probability?' and 'Consequences?'). Then, against the corresponding disaster, enter some kind of score or your conclusions into the relevant column.

At this point, you're probably thinking; *"This is all fine, but I don't happen to have a crystal ball handy! How on Earth can anyone know what's going to happen in the next five years?"* Well, nobody can, but at least it is possible to make some educated guesses. Watch the news, read the newspapers, listen to the radio, and search the Internet. In other words, **keep your eyes and ears open** and **do some research. Figure out what is trending** and how it could somehow jeopardize your safety. Remember to focus mainly on the crises that are most likely to occur in your local area.

At the very least, take a few minutes and **consider your location**. Open a map and examine what geographical features and man-made facilities are within a 20 mile radius of your home and place of work (i.e. forests, rivers, dams, cities, airports, power stations, army bases, chemical plants, etc). **Think carefully about what could go wrong at these places** and how those problems could be detrimental to you and your family. Then **decide if there are any eventualities you ought to prepare for**.

For example, if you live by a river that regularly bursts its banks every hundred years or so, should you prepare for the next flood? If the last one took place only recently, it's probably not going to happen again anytime soon; but if the river hasn't flooded for nearly a century then maybe it's time to worry and prepare!

Of course, you could be unlucky here, decide to do nothing as the next flood isn't due for decades, and then lose everything when a freak storm bursts those banks just a year after the last deluge occurred. Equally, you could decide to spend thousands of dollars raising your house on to stilts only to find the river never floods again.

Nevertheless, consider the consequences. The worst that could happen in the last scenario is you'd waste a ton of money and be accused of over-reacting.

In the former, however, you'd lose your entire estate and could end up dead!

Ultimately, it's your call as to what you do regarding any potential threats in your area. But it is all too easy to get carried away by media hype and paranoia (remember that twaddle about the millennium bug causing World War III, or the mystical claptrap surrounding the Mayan apocalypse of 2012?). However, as my Mama used to say; "It's always better to be safe than sorry."

Obviously – and crucially – we need to get as much accurate information as possible as to when disaster is approaching. Below are a few points to consider.

How to Get Information on Impending Disasters

– Find out how your local authorities will notify you of an impending disaster and how to get information during the crisis. Examples include local radio, TV, or NOAA Weather Radio stations or channels.

– Learn the difference between the different types of weather alerts such as watches and warnings and what actions to take in each case.

– Know what actions to take in order to protect yourself during the disasters that may occur in the areas you live, work, travel to, or have recently moved to. For example, if you work in a place where earthquakes are common and you are unfamiliar with them, make sure you learn how to protect yourself should one occur. (The "10 Common Disasters and How to Deal with them" section, later in this book, will help you here).

– Share what you have learned with your family, household, and neighbors so you can encourage them to be informed.

Should I Stay or Should I Go?

Ok, you've sat down and worried yourself sick about every possible disastrous scenario. Then, after much hand wringing, you've finally calmed down and rationally devised your list of the *likely* disasters you might actually have to face. You have also found out how the authorities are going to let you know what is about to happen.

Now you have to figure out; "Should I stay or should I go? Do I even have to deal with this situation at all?" If you've been warned of an impending disaster, surely a much a better and safer alternative would be to get the heck outta there so you can find a nice, secure place until it all blows over!

In many situations this is absolutely the right thing to do. (The "10 Common Disasters and How to Deal with them" section of this book contains more guidance on this topic.)

But, if you are ordered by the authorities to stay indoors, do just that. Don't even think about leaving until you're given the "all-clear."

However, things are not often so clear-cut. Leaving your home, with the knowledge that it may not be there tomorrow is traumatic, to say the least. Moreover, you may worry that the warnings will turn out to be false alarms (particularly if it has happened before). But before you decide whether or not you can tear yourself away from your house, the stark reality is that you can replace a home and you can't buy a new life. Bear in mind that all disasters are, by their very definition, unpredictable. The challenges they present can become potentially lethal in a flash. Millions of victims of catastrophes have perished simply because they waited too long and didn't evacuate in time. (Remember those heart-breaking videos of the Japanese and Thai Tsunamis? Hopefully, you'll realize from these just how easy it is to be overtaken quickly by disastrous events.)

Even if you do decide to stay and survive the initial event, the aftermath could be almost as challenging. Although you can store provisions (as covered later in this book) to keep you alive and in good health for a few weeks, you need to be prepared for the possibility that you could be completely cut off from humanity for a while. You could even be living in a house that now has structural damage caused by the disaster. The power has probably been cut off too, depriving you and everyone else in the household of electricity for lighting, cooking, or heating. It is also unlikely that you have any fresh water from the mains for drinking or even basic sanitation. Most importantly, you could be far away from any professional medical assistance at a time when it might become sorely needed.

However, if you do decide to leave, please be aware that life will be extremely tough. You could be exposing yourself and your family to real deprivation while on the road and even to the very danger you're trying to flee from.

Where Is Everybody? How to Get Everyone Together Before You Leave

Not all your family members may be together when a disaster occurs, so you will need to try to gather them as soon as possible.

The first step is to make sure everyone can contact one another and that they all know the prearranged meeting point.

Therefore, check that everyone's cell phone is programmed with everyone else's numbers, that they are fully charged, and that any payments have been made.

Additionally, **program the phones** with the numbers and details of out-of-town **relatives or friends**, so they can be contacted if anything happens to you.

Even if the cell networks break down, the phones will still be useful as electronic address books as they will contain everyone's contact information (remember to also supply your family with extra chargers, preferably with some sort of battery back-up). If possible, **always provide alternative landline and mobile numbers** in case any are in use or a service is down.

The reason I mention this is because if you have difficulty getting through on your mobile phone, you might have better luck sending text messages or making long distance calls. The latter bypasses any local phone lines that may have become overloaded or been put out of commission by the disaster. Since, the text messaging services use the more "primitive" parts of the cell network, they might still keep running, even if the vocal call "parts" have given up the ghost!

It is also a good idea, to provide everyone with a good old-fashioned **paper address book**, containing all of the above information, in case the phones are lost or there is nowhere to charge them.

If any family members are within walking distance (or if the disaster involves the home, such as in an indoor fire), **pre-arrange to meet them in front of your house or close by**, but far enough to ensure safety and be away from the danger. Preferably, choose a spot near some lighting (such as a street lamp). During the darkness of night, this makes it easy to tell right away if anyone is missing.

If any members are too far away to reach your home, arrange to pick them up outside, but as **close as possible to your neighborhood**. (The longer you are apart from them the harder it will be for you to catch up with them later.)

Therefore, it's a good idea to prearrange this meeting point. Just in case this location is unexpectedly caught up in the disaster, be sure to provide family members with **several alternatives**, further out from your neighborhood.

Hopefully, there will be some family members who are already safely out of the area (perhaps someone is out of town on business or on vacation far from the crisis). In this case, leave them where they are, but inform them where you are going as soon as you can. They may feel compelled to join you, but advise them only to do so if they are 100 percent certain they will not put themselves in danger by trying to get there.

You can let your family and friends know how you are doing by registering online with the **Safe and Well website** (https://safeandwell.communityos.org/cms/index.php). The American Red Cross runs this facility and, alternatively, you can register over the phone by calling 1-800-RED CROSS (1-800-733-2767) then selecting the prompt for "Disaster."

Once everyone is together, it's time to swing into action with your evacuation plan.

Not done one yet? Note sure what to do? Then read on and all will be revealed!

The Evacuation Plan

1. Figure out how to get out.

You should start by **brainstorming the best ways to get out of your house**. Make sure *all* your family members, young, old, able bodied, or disabled – and your pets – can get out in the dark and that there are at least two escape routes out of the building that are unhindered by obstacles or junk. (Needless to say the more cluttered or untidy your home is, the harder it is to leave in a hurry. Maybe it's time to clear out the clutter!) You may, also need to give **special consideration for the elderly or the disabled**, such as fitting hand rails or wheelchair ramps (removable or permanent) where ever steps are prevalent. One final suggestion is to have **plenty of flashlights** (preferably, the LED type) ready to hand out. (There's more information on these and other gadgets covered in the chapter about the **Emergency Preparedness Kit** later in this book).

2. Learn how to turn off the utilities.

The second step is to find out how to turn off all the home utilities in a hurry, especially the gas and electricity supplies (after all, why lay a booby trap for rescuers if they come, by turning your house into a bomb). Likewise, turn off any propane tanks you may have. Obviously use your common sense here – don't try turning off anything if the house is already ablaze or a massive wave is approaching!

3. Decide where you want to go.

Once everything is off and you are sure everyone can get out, you need to decide where to go. Put simply, attempt to go to **public shelters first**. If that's not suitable or possible, **try to stay with people you know**. If that's not an option, **rent a place**.

Let's take a look at these options in a bit more detail:

3.1. Find your nearest public shelters.

The next step is to check to **see what shelters or other "safe houses" are available in your area** (i.e. speak to the local police, the American Red Cross, or National Guard to see places they suggest). Note that not only is this the simplest solution, it is also the quickest. This is important because the quicker you get yourself and your family to a place of safety the better.

3.2. Make arrangements with friends and relatives.

Alternatively, arrange to **stay with friends or family members** who are **located securely from the crisis**, if possible. Preferably this location should be at least 75 to 150 miles away and in a different setting i.e. if you live on the coast, make sure they are well inland; if you're on a flood plain, make sure they are located on high ground etc.

3.3 Stay in rental accommodations.

If all else fails, you may need to **find hotels/motels or hostels**, or if you own a caravan it could be **a lot in a trailer park**. Be aware however, that many others will be doing the same and it could become very difficult to find accommodations in such circumstances.

Moreover, you may need to pay a premium price for these, even if you do find a place to stay. However, don't give up. Though it may be a little discouraging, eventually you will find somewhere to stay and at least you will be safe.

3.4. Find pet-friendly accommodations (if you have pets).

Most public shelters do not allow pets on their premises, so you will need to **find animal-friendly alternatives**. For full details on these and much more, please refer to the "Special Considerations" chapter later in this book.

3.5 Check that you've done everything right so far.

Wherever you decide to go, **make sure it really is "safe"** and **practical to get to**. This may seem unbelievably obvious, but it is amazing how many people simply "head for the hills" in times of crisis and end up stuck on a freeway in jeopardy.

4. Decide how to get there.

How you get to your destination is up to you, but by far **the best option is by car**. Your car provides a ready-made, mobile shelter and, of course, a place to store your luggage. Moreover, you're guaranteed to keep at least some of your family members together with you during the emergency. If you don't have your own vehicle, then if possible, try to hitch a ride with a neighbor, family member, or friend. Bear in mind that **public transportation may well be badly disrupted** and manhandling your possessions on an overcrowded bus, train, or plane packed with panicky passengers, is no fun at all.

4.1. Check that your car is ready for the journey.

If you are going by car, it's a good idea **to make sure your "safe house" is accessible on one tank of gas**. Everyone else may have the same idea, so there's a good chance many gas stations along your route will run dry as people fill up their automobiles while fleeing from the emergency.

There's no point in even attempting to make the journey if your vehicle is not up to the task. Make sure that **everything mechanical** is up and running (i.e. there's plenty of gas in the tank, the tires and the spare are pumped up, the battery is okay, there's enough water in the radiator, the oil levels topped-up etc.) and make sure you have **plenty of blankets** and some form of **emergency preparedness kit** with you in case you breakdown (more on that later).

4.2. Figure out the best routes to your destination.

Central to this is **route planning**. Spot any potential hazards or bottlenecks on your route. If possible, **devise several alternative routes. Memorize these** and take a stack of **maps** along with you. You can also use these to improvise alternatives, just in case accidents or other issues halt your progress. Program your destination into your **GPS**, but **don't totally rely on it**. These devices can take you through some very strange routes indeed and sometimes lose their signal in very poor weather conditions, as their satellite links become temporarily lost.

When planning your travel, include a **fast, direct route** that you can use to "beat the rush" and a **"back-woods" alternative** in case everyone else has thought of the above and clogged the interstates up into a deadlock.

4.3. Make sure they really are the best routes.

The **American Red Cross** suggests that you **practice your evacuation plan twice a year** and **test-drive the routes** for viability. This may seem a little over-the-top, but if you live in an area that is prone to natural disasters, then it is essential you follow their advice. It is also advisable to **attempt** your **test-drives in two opposing seasons**, (i.e. summer and winter) to see the different obstacles you might face. You might encounter unexpected traffic problems because swarms of vacationers clog the roads during the summer. Alternatively, you may find, to your horror, that many of the roads on your "fast" route become impassable or can even be "closed" completely by the authorities during the winter months. You won't discover any of this until you try those routes.

The Emergency Preparedness Kit (Bug-Out Bag)

The emergency preparedness kits (also known as the bug-out bags) should be the first (and probably the only) things you'll need when it's time to bail out.

When there's an emergency, like a house fire or visit from a canvassing politician, grab the kids, grab the bags, and get the heck outta there!

The bug-out bags are there to provide everything you'll need to survive for a short period of time while you're on the road (both figuratively and literally) or for the longer periods when trapped at home.

How long these bags keep you supplied depends on how long you wish to prepare for, and, of course, whether the bags need to be carried. However, at a **bare minimum**, you should have at least **three days' worth of provisions packed in each bag**.

Don't get carried away though. Emergency situations can change dramatically and unexpectedly. There may be cases where you planned to stay put in your home, only to find later that you need to evacuate in a hurry. Therefore, as your family may need to carry their bags for a while, pack them according to what each member is capable of handling. There's no point in stuffing a 20 pound kit into a bag if you intend it to be carried by a five-year-old boy or an eighty-year-old granny with osteoporosis!

As you might have gathered by now, **each family member should have their own bag**. Each bag should be tailored to their individual needs and labelled accordingly. For example, if one of your children is diabetic, **keep all medications in that child's specific bug-out bag**. In the case of medicines however, be sure to keep a tight reign over them and don't allow any of your little ones to touch any bag unless it is their own.

Now we come to the thorny issue of what to actually put in these bags.

What You Need In a Bug-Out Bag

You can buy ready-made kits over the Internet, but they will need additional items added by you in order to tailor them to your needs. Often, they come at a premium price, too and may contain items you'll probably never use or ones you already own.

However, you can make your own kits for less and they will be far more suitable for your purposes. The first thing to do is to get a hold of some brightly colored backpacks or water-resistant duffle bags with shoulder straps. Why brightly colored you ask? So, you can see them more clearly and easily in the dark!

The Basic Checklist

It is all manner of advice as to what to put in these bags, but below is a checklist of the basic provisions you'll need, courtesy of the American Red Cross:

– Water: one gallon per-person, per-day (3-day supply for evacuation, 2-week supply for home)

– Food: non-perishable, easily prepared items (3-day supply for evacuation, 2-week supply for home)

– Flashlight

– Battery powered or hand cranked radio (NOAA Weather Radio, if possible)

– Extra batteries

– First aid kit (more on that later)

– Medications (7-day supply) and medical items

– Multi-purpose tool such as a Swiss Army Knife

– Sanitation and personal hygiene items

– Copies of essential personal documents (medication lists, additional prescriptions and any pertinent medical information, proof-of-address, deeds/leases, passports, birth certificates and insurance policies)

– Cell phones with chargers

– Family and emergency contact information

– Extra cash

– Emergency blanket

– Map(s) of the area

Here are a few others you should consider:

– A change of heavy duty clothes

– An old pair of comfortable walking shoes

– A spare pair of spectacles if needed

– A manual can opener

– A big box of waterproof matches (expensive but worth it!)

– A roll of duct tape (you'll be amazed how useful this stuff is!)

– Candles

– Pet food

– Baby supplies (bottles, formula, baby food and diapers)

You could include some kind of camping stove, but you will obviously need to carry this along, and eventually forage for, hard-to-come-by fuel. This just makes for more to lug around in your kit and it could even become a potential fire hazard if butane canisters are ever damaged in transit.

Now, let's go over some of these points in a little more detail:

Water and Storage

By far, **water is the single most important item you will need**, because you won't survive longer than 3 days without it (maybe only 24 hours in a desert climate). You'll need to maintain daily hydration to keep yourself healthy.

For portable "bug-out bags," the best bet is to buy the small (300 - 500ml) water bottles, rather than the larger sizes, so you can drink straight from them and not bother with cups or beakers. Additionally, they are very tough and won't "implode" unlike the bigger bottles. As these bottles are so compact, they can be easily scattered around the insides of your bags or backpack, and thus store more efficiently.

To supplement the supply in your bug-out bag, stuff any spare freezer space, with PET bottles filled with water (the kind liters of soda come in). Besides providing additional drinking water, the ice formed can help keep refrigerated food cool during a power outage.

All About Food

You can survive without food for much longer than water – maybe up-to a month – but in an emergency situation, it is crucial to keep your strength up by eating healthy and as regularly as possible.

THE CALORIE TABLE

The table below provides a rough guide to an average person's daily caloric needs.

Age in years / Calories per day

1–3   (male) 1,230   (female) 1,165

4–6   (male) 1,715   (female) 1,545

7–10   (male) 1,970   (female) 1,740

11–14 (male) 2,220   (female) 1,845

15–18 (male) 2,755   (female) 2,110

19+ (Adult) (male) 2,550   (female) 1,940

The calorific requirements, for both sexes, reduce past the age of 51. Consequently, moderately active seniors require between 2200 and 1800 calories per day respectively for men and women.

I referred to this as a "rough guide" earlier because an individual's build, weight, general health, and physical fitness level can all greatly influence their nutritional needs.

Moreover, these requirements may rise sharply during a crisis.

THE FOOD CALORIE CALCULATOR

None of the above means very much if you do not know the calorific values of the things you eat. There are literally thousands of different foods out there and to list all of them and their nutritional values would be impractical for this book. Fortunately, there are many calculators on the web that can provide this information. One of the best is at http://www.webmd.com/diet/healthtool-food-calorie-counter.

WHAT'S THE BEST FOOD TO TAKE?

Obviously, you can't freeze or chill foods on the road. Anything that can go bad or spoil quickly, such as bread or fresh milk, must be avoided. Additionally, any other foods that naturally harbor harmful bacteria should not be included (such as fresh eggs, pork, or poultry because these can easily become infected with Salmonella, E-coli, Listeria, etc.). Your only options, therefore, are non-perishable foods.

WHAT ARE NON-PERISHABLE FOODS?

Non-perishable foods are basically, any foods that are dried or canned. Choose those that are easily transportable. These should include at least one item from each of the following food groups (the greater the variety the better):

FRUITS AND VEGETABLES

Eating canned or dried fruits and vegetables will keep up your fiber, vitamin, and mineral levels, as well as help stave off illnesses – particularly important when you're under stress.

– Canned mixed vegetables

– Tomatoes (Canned in their own juice or in sauce)

– Canned fruit and fruit cups (again in their own juice)

- Dried fruit

- Jarred preserves such as strawberry jelly

CARBOHYDRATES

Carbohydrate provides your body with the daily energy it needs to keep going.

- Canned pasta

- Canned potatoes

- Canned rice

- Jar of honey

PROTEINS

Canned meats provide fuel for muscle tissue. Beans are great because, not only are they full of protein, they are a great source of fiber which is vital in maintaining good bowel health. They are also a lot cheaper than meat!

- Corned beef, spam, pork, any fish (especial oily like sardines), or chicken

- Bean soups

- Baked beans

- Any other dried and canned beans and peas

- Peanut butter

All the above can be eaten without pre-heating or cooking. Granted, some will taste pretty horrible when cold, but at least they will keep you fed and healthy.

FREEZE-DRIED PRODUCTS

Canned products are not the only option, especially since they do have a couple of drawbacks: their high weight and bulkiness. Freeze-dried products, on the other hand, are super light compared to cans and they take up very little space. However, they have drawbacks too. Freeze-dried foods can be very expensive for the small portions they provide and, of course, they will need re-hydrating with boiled water before they can be eaten. Not only will this put a strain on your water reserves, it will require you to take a portable stove along with you, too.

SNACKS

A good idea is to pack quick snacks, such as bags of peanuts, into any spare pockets you might have. These are great for staving off hunger and for providing some welcome relief from what may become a very boring, repetitive diet.

In addition to the above, I'd also recommend taking a couple of big bottles of multi-vitamins along for the trip. These can help supplement your diet, if you're running low on supplies or have small children or senior citizens to look after.

Remember, if you're traveling you might be able to top off your provisions along the way, but the choices may be very limited and expensive.

A Note About MRE's

You could also buy MRE's (meals ready to eat) which are field rationed packs that are similar to those consumed by the U.S. military and beloved by survivalists everywhere. These are very portable, convenient, and have a long shelf life of up to ten years.

There are a few downsides to them however. Often, they are freeze-dried so you'll need to add boiling water before they can be eaten. Also, MRE's are high in calories and salt because they are tailored for active combat troops who tend to burn off lots of energy and easily lose sodium through excessive sweating.

Consequently, these rations often contain poor levels of dietary fiber, so they can lead to constipation (particularly in IBS sufferers). Their saltiness can cause excessive thirst, which is bad news when water supplies are limited. Moreover, MRE's can cost a fortune if they're consumed daily.

Perhaps, worst of all, is that these MRE's are not very nice to eat! Some are so bad that they even have their own nicknames. For example, the frankfurters, which came in pouches of four, were referred, by troops, as "the four fingers of death." A fantastically sardonic comment on the "bowl un-friendless" of MRE's, was made at a USO show during the recent Iraq war. Comedian Al Franken joked that although he had eaten five of them, "None, so far, had an exit strategy!"

Flashlights, Radios, etc.

It's best to use LED flashlights or lanterns as they are more rugged and much more efficient than traditional lamps. In fact, they are so efficient, that some can even be hand-cranked and do not need batteries at all.

As my daughter would say, "batteries suck" and I kind of agree. They can be expensive, leak everywhere, take up space, weigh a lot, and always seem to die just when you really need them. Therefore, I recommend, if possible, buying hand-cranked (wind-up) lamps and radios (make sure those receivers can pick up NOAA Weather Radio so you can keep an ear on what Mother Nature might be up to).

Nowadays, you can even purchase "wind-up" multi-functional devices with built-in flashlights, radios, digital clocks, and miniature solar panels to help keep them charged. The benefits of these gadgets are obvious, but the phrase "Jack of all trades, master of none" may apply as does the saying, "Never put all your eggs in one basket." It's a good idea, therefore, to take a spare flashlight along just in case your multi-function device breaks or you find it isn't completely fit for your purposes. (In a pinch, you might manage without a radio, but you'll find it very tough to survive without some form of lighting).

Whatever you buy, never skimp on quality; always purchase the best you can afford. If you can, always try to look at a few customer reviews on the product before you part with your cash. Being able to see in the dark is crucial to your survival, so make sure you get a light that is tough enough for you to depend on it. Knowing what's happening in the crisis can also be a lifesaver, so get a decent radio. Remember that, although you may have an in-car stereo, it won't be much use if you're indoors, if your vehicle runs out of gas, or if the battery goes dead.

First Aid Kit

You should already have one of these in your home. You should also have one in your car (driving is a potential disaster in itself!) First aid kits can be bought anywhere and come in a bewildering verity of sizes and types. Below is what the American Red Cross recommends should be in yours (first aid kits can be purchased from their stores or chapters):

- 2 absorbent compress dressings (5 x 9 inches)

- 25 adhesive bandages (assorted sizes)

- 1 adhesive cloth tape (10 yards x 1 inch)

- 5 antibiotic ointment packets (approximately 1 gram)

- 5 antiseptic wipe packets

- 2 packets of aspirin (81 mg each)

- 1 blanket (space blanket)

- 1 breathing barrier (with one-way valve)

- 1 instant cold compress

- 2 pair of non-latex gloves (size: large)

- 2 hydrocortisone ointment packets (approximately 1 gram each)

- Scissors

- 1 roller bandage (3 inches wide)

- 1 roller bandage (4 inches wide)

- 5 sterile gauze pads (3 x 3 inches)

- 5 sterile gauze pads (4 x 4 inches)

- Oral thermometer (non-mercury/non-glass)

- 2 triangular bandages

- Tweezers

- First aid instruction booklet

Cash and Credit Cards

Many ATM's may not be working or will be drained of cash by evacuees. You'll therefore need some greenbacks! As a rule of thumb, if you can afford it, $500 should be enough to tie you over for a while. A spare credit card, would come in very handy for paying for accommodations or for withdrawing money if you eventually find a working ATM.

Emergency Blankets

What we are talking about here aren't just any old blankets that can get damp, smelly and take up space. These are those compact, expendable, foil 'jobs' used by the emergency service organizations. They often come in handy, multi-packs and are very cheap to buy (Amazon are currently selling 52" by 84" blankets for $1.49 each). In my view, they are an absolute essential for both keeping warm and for treating shock victims – a very probable situation after a disaster.

Everything I've discussed above covers what to do when you evacuate. However there are many occasions when you can't leave your house and you just have to tough it out. Let's find out how to cope in this situation.

The Shelter-in-Place Plan

"Shelter-in-place" means to take immediate shelter where you are – at home, work, school, or anywhere in between.

Fortunately, many of the things we covered earlier in our evacuation plan apply here as well.

In the case of the "bug-out bag", you merely stuff enough provisions in there so it can last a minimum of two weeks.

As you are in your own home, however, you'll have the benefit of all that additional space at your disposal. (We'll be covering how to use this effectively later in the "Long-Term Storage" section of this book.)

Below are some additional things to consider:

– Choose a room in advance for your shelter. The best is one with as few windows and doors as possible. A large room, preferably with a water supply, is desirable—something like a master bedroom, connected to a bathroom (there is more about house preparation later in the "10 Common Disasters and How to Deal with Them" chapter).

– Find out when warning systems are tested in your area. While testing is happening, determine whether you can hear or see sirens and/or warning lights from your home.

– Regularly practice your disaster plans with your family.

– Regularly check your **emergency preparedness kit** to be sure that everything is in order and that it is fully stocked.

– Contact workplaces, schools, nursing homes, or any other public places where your family may be. Ask about their "shelter-in-place" plans. Also contact your local town or city officials to find out about their approach to shelter-in-place plans.

How will I know when I need a "shelter-in-place"?

Your local police and/or fire department should contact you. Their warning procedures should include:

– "All-Call" telephoning system – an automated system for sending recorded messages (This is often referred to as "Reverse 911.")

– Emergency Alert System (EAS) broadcasts on radio or television

– Outdoor warning sirens or horns

– News media sources – radio, television, and cable

– NOAA Weather Radio alerts

– Residential route alerting – a fancy name for announcements made from vehicles with public address systems

Facilities that handle potentially dangerous materials, such as chemical installations and nuclear power stations, are required to install sirens and other warning systems (flashing warning lights) that cover a 10 mile radius around the plant. If these go off, be prepared for a stay-in-place warning.

Long-Term Storage

Although a disaster may have passed, the aftermath could present some serious challenges. It could take weeks before the local stores are stocked again. When they are, you may find prices, for even basic goods, cripplingly high.

It could take just as long to get the utilities back on. Therefore, you need to be prepared for this delay before you can once again enjoy the luxury of gas, electricity, or water flowing through your pipes.

You may need to feed visiting friends, caught in the disaster, or neighbors having difficulty after the event (this is not a time to be selfish – how would you feel if you were starving and your neighbor was refusing to share extra food?).

Therefore, you need to prepare for such eventualities in the months ahead.

Water

How much do I <u>really</u> need?

The American Red Cross advises that the average person requires one gallon of water a day to survive. This may seem plenty, but since this includes all of your drinking water as well, there really won't be much left over for other purposes. Therefore, I'd actually suggest having twice this amount. After a disaster, it is vital to maintain an adequate hygiene regime to help prevent disease. So, that additional gallon will become a necessity. Moreover, you will have twice the water for the preparation of freeze-dried foods or MRE's, if you have them.

How Do I Store It?

A handy way of acquiring large quantities of the wet stuff is to purchase one gallon jugs of the commercially produced, purified water. These have a shelf life of about two years. These can be bought very cheaply indeed – a box of six will only set you back about three dollars (check out the Internet for suppliers). The boxes are made of heavy-duty cardboard that protects the jugs from rupturing and allows for easy stacking.

If you prefer to store ordinary tap water, avoid using milk cartons! It's practically impossible to remove the milky residue from them and your water will quickly become unsafe to drink. For a similar reason, never use bleach bottles. The bleach leeches in and out of the plastic in surprisingly concentrated quantities, so much so, that even the manufacturers don't recommend you use them for this purpose.

For storing of large quantities of water, you're probably better off using containers of at least 5 gallon capacity. Commercial food grade plastic canisters are ideal and come in all shapes and sizes from 5 to 250 gallons or more. Don't get carried away buying the biggest, however. You may need to move your container and you will certainly need a hand pump to get out the water from anything over a 50 gallon capacity.

How Do I Purify It?

As the shortages drag on, your drinking water may start to turn cloudy. A soon as you notice this – purify it! Boiling it for thirty minutes is an effective means, but this method takes an awful lot of fuel and wastes precious water as steam. A better method is to use filtration units. Many require hand pumping, although the best use gravity filtration alone. Both of these units have a limited capacity and can be expensive. Although "cleansing preparations" are commercially available, the cheapest and most effective purification option is to pour a little household bleach into your drinking water. However, be sure to use it very sparingly; about 1-2 teaspoon for every 10 gallons of water is all you will need, depending upon its murkiness. Make sure you only use pure bleach; avoid any tainted with fancy colorants or perfumes!

WATER CONSERVATION

Once you're in a survival situation, conservation becomes a necessity. While water for drinking is crucial, you may need it for re-hydrating dried foods as well. Water from boiling pasta, vegetables etc., should be kept and used for drinking after it has cooled. Retain the liquid from canned vegetables too. You may be tempted to draw water from local streams, lakes etc. Be *very* wary, however, because dirty water can kill you! All types of nasty diseases may very well be lurking in it, particularly in the aftermath of a disaster. If you do decide to risk it, thoroughly sieve and purify the water before you use it at all.

Food

HOW MUCH FOOD DO I NEED?

The American Red Cross suggests you store a minimum of a two week supply of food, but an awful lot depends on the types of disasters you are likely to face. Therefore, always plan for the longest probable crises you may encounter. You can never be sure how much you are going to need, so always overestimate your requirements.

As you will be storing non-perishable items, none will go to waste. You can always top-off your pantry by "dipping in" to your stash. Just, be sure to replenish your emergency supplies as soon as you use them. This rotation will keep things as fresh as possible.

Economics is another important consideration. Food prices invariably rise because of inflation. If crop yields falter (a more regular occurrence through global warming), the prices rise even more sharply. Therefore, keeping a large stash of non-perishable food not only makes sense for emergency preparation; it also makes sense for your wallet!

(As a guide, here's what I do. As my family lives in a storm prone area, we stash six to eight weeks' worth of food in the basement. Some of our neighbors, however, store over three months' worth. It all comes down to your budgetary limits and how much space you have.)

FOOD STORAGE CALCULATORS

There are hundreds of special food storage calculators that can be found and purchased over the Internet. These can help determine what provisions you'll need to support your family for up to a year. Note, however, that most are based on an original application provided by The Church of Latter Day Saints. Much of what they suggest is very sensible, but it does assume you can cook. Some of the recommendations are a little "odd," too. (Salad dressing? Mayonnaise? These are emergency provisions, right?)

The original "LDS" calculator can be found at: http://lds.about.com/library/bl/faq/blcalculator.htm

A spreadsheet version can be downloaded here: http://foodstoragemadeeasy.net/fsme/docs/foodstoragecalculator.xls

WHAT FOODS DO I STORE?

Fortunately, we covered most of this earlier in the chapter entitled "What's the Best Food to Take?" The biggest, difference here is in the quantities you'll need to keep. To recap:

– Store only non-perishable foods.

– Try to avoid those that take a lot of cooking or need re-hydrating.

– Store a variety of foods in each of the following three groups: fruits and vegetables (canned or dried), proteins (canned meat, beans etc.) and carbohydrates (canned potatoes, rice, pasta, etc.).

– Don't bother with MRE's. These are really only for use when "on the road" and have a number of drawbacks – like causing health issues and needing re-hydration.

FOOD ROTATION

This is an important consideration. Most canned foods have a shelf life of up to a year and for some, it can be as long as 18 months or more. These products won't actually "go bad," if kept for longer, but they will become less palatable and nutritious as their vitamin and mineral content "depletes" over time.

It's therefore essential that you rotate their use, by storing and consuming your cans in order of expiration date (i.e. stack the older ones in front of the newer ones and use those first). If any are devoid of expiry information, assume the worst and consume them within a year. An alternative method is to mark your cans with consecutive numbers as you purchase them, then open those with the lowest numbers first.

If you have a particularly large stash, it's a good idea to replace 20 to 25 percent of it every few months or so. This ensures nothing sits for longer than it should. Consume the foods you remove immediately or donate them to a local charity.

One final note: make sure your cans are well protected and kept dry. If they become punctured in any way, the food inside will almost certainly be rotten by the time you open it. Therefore, check that your cans are undamaged before you use them. (The odd dent is okay, but if you see any leakage – chuck it!)

Special Considerations

How to Deal with Your Kids in an Emergency

Many disasters can happen in a flash and without warning. They are scary for us adults, but downright traumatic for children, especially if they don't know what to do or who to turn to.

During a crisis, you may have to leave your home and depart from your daily routine. Unfortunately, a child's sense of security depends on these things. They wake up, have breakfast, go to school, play with friends, and watch TV (probably too much!). When disasters interrupt these routines, many children become worried and frightened.

During crisis situations, children will look to you and other adults for guidance and reassurance. They'll also copy your behavior. If you are scared, then they will believe there must be a good reason to be afraid, and so they become anxious themselves. If you appear overcome with a sense of loss, your child will feel this more strongly, as well. Negative emotions are contagious. Fortunately, so are positive emotions so try your best to be hopeful and remain as calm as possible.

However, don't be too hard on yourself if your "mask" slips at times. Feelings of fear are healthy and natural for everyone; you are only human after all. But as an adult, you need to keep on top of the situation. When you're sure that danger has passed, concentrate on the emotional needs of your child or children. Ask them what is concerning them the most and provide comfort and reassurance to ease these worries. Give back to your children a sense of control by getting them to participate in the family's recovery activities. This will also help them to not dwell on things, as well as encourage the belief that life may soon get back to "normal."

Always be aware that how you respond during this time could have a lasting impact on how your children will develop as adults.

Children's imaginations can also run wild at these times. This often leads them to develop exaggerated fears and concerns which could even lead to phobic behavior in later life. Therefore, you must take these feelings seriously. Remember that a child who feels afraid *is* afraid. They will need your words and actions to provide comfort and support. When talking with your child, be sure to present a realistic picture that is both honest and manageable.

Help with the Disabled During an Emergency

– Ask about any special local assistance programs for the disabled available in the event of an emergency in your area. Many communities ask disabled people to register, usually with the local fire or police departments or with the local emergency management office, so that help can be provided quickly in times of disaster. If your family member has a personal care attendant, be sure to tell that person if they are already registered and with whom.

– If their disability is one that classifies them as electric-dependent (i.e. an oxygen tank, etc.), be sure to register the disabled person with your local utility company.

– If they use an electric wheelchair or scooter, have a manual wheelchair available for backup.

– Learn how to deal with any specialty equipment and get advice from their care worker about how to handle them during an emergency.

– Label equipment and attach laminated instructions for equipment use.

– Store back-up equipment (mobility, medical, etc.) at your neighbor's home, school, or your workplace.

– Check that their care assistant's agency has special provisions for emergencies or provides them with another location should an evacuation be ordered.

What to Do about Your Pets in an Emergency

1. Find accommodations for them.

You may be asking by now, "What about **my pets**? Do I really need to leave them behind?" The short answer is "no" as long as you are aware that, for public health reasons, **most emergency shelters will not allow pets on their premises**. You will therefore need to keep a **contact list** of **pet-friendly hotels, motels, veterinary services**, and **animal shelters** that are along your evacuation route. This may make your search for accommodations a little tougher. But remember, your pets are part of the family too! If you do have difficulty coping with them, get your pets to the nearest safe location as soon as you can. You can always reunite with them once the crisis is over.

2. Build a Pet Emergency Preparedness Kit.

Your pet's essential items should be kept in something strong, easily portable, and accessible such as a duffle bag or covered trash container. Your pet emergency preparedness kit should include:

– Medications and medical records (store these in a waterproof pouch)

– A Pet First Aid kit (These are similar to human kits, but better suited to our furry friends. You can purchase these online for about $20.)

– A pair of sturdy leashes, harnesses, and/or a pet-carrier to transport them safely and stop your animals from escaping

– Up-to-date photos of your animals, just in case they get lost

– Food, drinkable water, bowls, cat litter, and litter box

– A manual can opener

– Documentation about feeding times, medical conditions, or behavioral problems (Also include the name and contact details of your veterinarian in case you have to foster or board your pets.)

– Your pet's bed and/or toys (Make sure there easily transportable and can be carried in your bags.)

What to Do If Your Pets are Left Behind

Unfortunately, there may be circumstances in which you have to leave your pets behind at home. There's still hope for them, though, if you inform the emergency services they are there. The ASPCA recommends using a rescue sticker alert to let rescue workers know that pets are inside your premises. Make sure the sticker is clearly visible and marked with the types and number of pets in the building and your veterinarian's contact number.

If you've managed to successfully escape with your pets (if you have time), write "EVACUATED" across the stickers. This prevents rescue workers wasting their efforts searching for pets that are no longer there.

10 Common Disasters and How to Deal with Them

Space dictates that I can't cover every crisis here, but this section provides a quick guide on how to deal with some of the most common emergency disasters that can take place in the United States.

1. Earthquakes

These are amazingly common in the United States. No fewer than 45 territories, in every region are at a moderate to very high risk of earthquakes.

Caused by the cracking and shifting of rock beneath the earth's crust, earthquakes can strike suddenly, at any time, and often without warning.

1.1. PREPARATION

– Learn the fire evacuation and earthquake plans of any building you regularly occupy, such as your home, office, school, church etc.

– Choose safe hiding places in each of these surroundings, such as under sturdy furniture or against interior walls away from windows or anything that could fall on you.

– Practice the "drop, cover, and hold-on" strategy in these places. If your furniture is unsuitable, sit on the floor next to an interior wall and cover your head and neck with your arms.

– Keep a flashlight and sturdy shoes by everyone's bed to prepare for night-time quakes.

– Check that your home is strongly anchored to its foundation.

– Securely, bolt and brace water heaters, gas appliances, and all tall furniture to wall studs.

– Hang heavy items, such as pictures and mirrors, away from places where people might sit or sleep.

– Brace all overhead light fixtures.

– Fit sturdy latches or bolts on cabinets. Make sure large or heavy items are stored closest to the floor.

– Learn your local seismic building standards and land use codes before starting any new construction.

1.2. How to Respond (Indoors)

– STAY INSIDE! (There's a far greater chance of being killed by falling masonry, then a building collapse).

– Drop, cover, and hold on. Keep as still as possible.

– If you are in bed stay there, curl up, and hold on. Protect your head with a pillow.

– Stay away from windows to avoid being injured or cut by shattering glass.

– When the shaking stops and you are sure it is safe, leave the building via the stairs. Avoid using elevators in case of aftershocks, power outages, etc.

1.3. How to Respond (Outdoors)

– Find a clear spot, away from buildings, power lines, trees, streetlights, etc.

– Drop to the ground.

– Stay down until the shaking stops.

– If you are in a vehicle, pull over and stop at the nearest clear location. Try to avoid bridges, overpasses, and power lines. Stay in the car with your seatbelt fastened until the quake subsides. Then drive, carefully, avoiding bridges and ramps if possible. (The damage to these may not be obvious but they can still easily collapse.)

– If a power line falls on your vehicle, DON'T GET OUT! Wait for assistance.

– Earthquakes often trigger landslides. If driving in a mountainous area or near unstable slopes or cliffs, look out for falling rocks and/or debris.

2. House Fires

The most effective way to prevent house fires is to remove all fire hazards from your home. Sixty-five percent of house fire deaths occur in homes with no working smoke detectors. During a fire, effective alarms and a regularly practiced evacuation plan can save lives.

2.1 PREPARATION

– Keep flammable items at least three feet away from anything hot, such as heaters.

– Don't smoke in bed.

– Regularly talk to your children about the dangers of fire, matches, and lighters. Always keep these out of the reach of your children.

– Turn off all portable heaters when you leave the room or go to sleep.

2.1.1. INSTALL SMOKE DETECTORS

– Mount these on each level of your house, as well as inside and outside all bedrooms.

– Teach your children what the alarm sounds like and what to do if they hear it.

– Every month, check that each detector is working by pushing the test button.

– Replace the batteries in each detector at least once a year. In the meantime, if the alarm chirps, its battery is low and it needs immediate changing.

– Replace your smoke detectors every 10 years. Never disable these or your carbon monoxide alarms.

– Carbon monoxide alarms are not substitutes for smoke detectors. Learn the difference between their sounds.

2.1.2. INSTALL CARBON MONOXIDE ALARMS

– Mount these in central locations on every level of your home and outside bedrooms.

– If an alarm sounds, quickly move outside or near an open window or door.

– Never use a generator, grill, camp stove, or any other fuel-burning device inside partially or fully enclosed areas of your home.

2.1.3. COOKING SAFELY

– Stay in the kitchen when frying, grilling, or broiling. If leaving your home, even for short periods of time, always turn off the stove.

– Stay at home while simmering, baking, roasting, or boiling. Check the food regularly and use a timer to remind yourself that it is cooking.

– Keep flammable items (potholders, towels, plastic, clothing, etc.) away from stoves.

– Keep your pets off cooking surfaces and countertops to prevent them from knocking things over and on to burners.

2.1.4. PLAN FOR EVACUATION

– Ensure each household member knows two methods of escape from every room of your house.

– Check that everyone knows where to meet other family members once you are outside during a fire.

– Practice your evacuation plan at least twice a year and at different times/seasons.

– Practice by waking up to the smoke alarm, floor crawling to escape, and meeting outside. Make sure everybody knows how to call 9-1-1.

– Teach everyone to STOP, DROP, and ROLL if their clothes ever catch on fire.

2.2. How to Respond

– GET OUT, STAY OUT, CALL 9-1-1 or another local emergency number.

– Follow your escape plan: Never open doors or handles that are warm to the touch – use your second way out instead.

– Crawl under smoke.

– Go to your outside meeting place. Call for help.

– If smoke, heat, or flames block your exit routes, stay in the room with doors closed. Place a wet towel under the door. Call the fire department or 9-1-1. Open a window and wave a brightly colored cloth or flashlight to signal for help.

2.2.1. How to Use Fire Extinguishers

Use fire extinguishers ONLY if you have been trained by the fire department and under the following conditions:

– The fire is confined to a small area and is not growing.

– The room is not smoke-filled.

– Everyone has exited the building.

– The fire department has been called.

– Remember the word PASS when using a fire extinguisher:

P – Pull the pin and hold the extinguisher with the nozzle pointing away from you.

A – Aim low. Point the extinguisher at the base of the fire.

S – Squeeze the lever slowly and evenly.

S – Sweep the nozzle from side to side.

3. Floods

While it's impossible to completely flood-proof a property, plenty can be done to reduce the damage caused by flooding.

Most importantly, prepare in advance; don't wait until flooding looks likely as you won't have time to buy supplies or put proper measures in place.

3.1. PREPARE (THE HOME)

Doors: Purchase purpose-built flood boards. Install them when flooding is imminent. You can also raise door thresholds.

Walls and floors: Install a damp-proof course, which is a horizontal barrier in a wall designed to resist moisture. Seal floors ('tanking') to prevent water rising through the ground.

Air bricks: Purchase these specially designed self-sealing covers to place over current air vents to block out flood water.

Drains and pipes: Fit non-return valves into drains, water inlets, and outlet pipes.

Shelving: Put valuable items on high-mounted shelves.

Audio-visual equipment: Mount this equipment on a wall about five-feet above ground level.

Baseboards: Install water-resistant baseboards or waterproof your current baseboards.

Pumps: Put one in a basement or an under-floor void (crawl space) to extract any water.

Walls: Use dry-line walls. Employ horizontal plasterboard or lime-based plaster instead of gypsum. Purchase a draining system for cavity walls.

Flooring: If possible, lay individual carpet squares rather than wall-to-wall carpeting. Always have extra carpet squares so that you can replace certain ones that are damaged after the flood is over.

Doors and windows: Install synthetic or waxed windows and doors or apply waterproofing stains or seals.

Kitchen and bathroom: Use water-resistant materials (stainless steel, plastic, etc.) and avoid chipboard/pressed wood. Where possible, raise appliances on plinths/platforms.

Electrical: Raise outlets, fuse boxes, switches, controls, and wiring at least five-feet above ground level. If rewiring, bring cables down the wall to the raised outlets so these are unaffected.

3.2. PREPARE (YOURSELF)

– Maintain an "emergency preparedness kit" (this is covered in the earlier "Bug-Out Bag chapter").

3.3. HOW TO RESPOND

– Check local radio, television stations, and NOAA Weather Radio for flood information from the National Weather Service (NWS).

– Be prepared to evacuate at a moment's notice.

– When a flood or flash flood warning is issued for your area, immediately head for higher ground and stay there.

– Avoid floodwaters. If you come upon a flowing stream deeper than your ankles, stop, turn around, and head in another direction. Just six inches of swift water can sweep you off your feet.

– While driving, if you encounter a flooded road, turn around and choose another route. If you are caught by flooding while driving and the waters are rising rapidly around you, vacate your car immediately and move to higher ground. Many vehicles are carried away by less than two feet of rapid-moving water.

– Keep children away from water. They can easily get into difficulty and the water may be contaminated.

– Be especially cautious at night when it is harder to recognize flood-related dangers.

– Standard homeowner's insurance policies do not cover flooding. Make sure you have additional coverage from weather conditions associated with floods, hurricanes, tropical storms etc. For more information, visit the National Flood Insurance Program website at www.FloodSmart.gov.

4. Heat Waves

In recent years, heat waves have caused more deaths than any other weather event, including flooding. A heat wave is defined as a prolonged period of excessive heat (generally 10 degrees or more above the average) that often causes extreme humidity.

People living in urban areas may be at a greater risk for heat waves than those living in rural areas, so be aware of this if you live in or near a city.

You may encounter local weather forecasters using the terms listed below when excessive heat is predicted. Listen for these during all the warmer months – not just the summer:

Excessive Heat Watch: The conditions are "right" for temperatures to reach or exceed local Excessive Heat Warning criteria in the next 24 to 72 hours.

Excessive Heat Warning: Heat Index values are forecasted to meet or exceed locally defined warning criteria for at least 2 days (daytime highs = 105 - 110° Fahrenheit).

Heat Advisory: Heat Index values are forecasted to meet locally defined advisory criteria for 1 to 2 days (daytime highs = 100 - 105° Fahrenheit).

The heat index (HI) is the temperature the body feels when the effects of air temperature (heat) and relative humidity are combined. Exposure to direct sunlight can increase this by as much as 15° F.

4.1. How to Prepare

– Tune in to your local weather forecasts and be aware of upcoming temperature changes.

– Be aware of both the temperature and the heat index.

– Discuss heat safety precautions with your household. Prepare plans for all of the places you spend time — home, work, school — and be ready for the possibility of power outages.

– Check the contents of your emergency preparedness kit in case a power outage occurs.

– Be prepared to help anyone in your neighborhood who is elderly, young, sick, or overweight as they are more likely to become victims of excessive heat.

– If you don't have air conditioning, stay in public places that may provide relief from the heat during the hottest part of the day (i.e. schools, libraries, theatres, and malls).

– Get trained in First Aid so you know how to treat heat-related emergencies.

– Ensure that your pets' needs for water and shade are fully met.

4.2. How to Respond

– Listen to a NOAA (National Oceanic and Atmospheric Administration) Weather Radio for critical updates from the National Weather Service (NWS).

– Never leave children or pets alone in enclosed vehicles.

– Stay hydrated. Drink plenty of fluids even if you don't feel thirsty. Avoid anything with caffeine or alcohol.

– Eat small meals, but consume food more often.

– Avoid extreme temperature changes.

– Wear loose-fitting, light-weight, light-colored clothing. Avoid dark colors as they absorb the sun's rays and make you feel hotter.

– Slow down, stay indoors, and avoid vigorous exercise during the hottest part of the day.

– Avoid outdoor games and activities.

– Use a" buddy system" when working in excessive heat.

– If you must work outdoors, take frequent breaks.

– Check on family, friends, and neighbors who don't have air conditioning, as well as those who live alone or who are more vulnerable to the effects of excessive heat.

– Frequently check on your pets to ensure that they are not too hot.

4.3. How to Treat Heat Related Medical Conditions

Heat waves can cause three heat-related conditions. Here's how to recognize and respond to them.

4.3.1. Heat cramps. These are muscular pains and spasms that usually occur in the legs or abdomen. Heat cramps are often an early indicator that the body is overheating.

– Move the victim to a cooler place and have them rest in a comfortable position. Lightly stretch the affected muscle and then gently massage that area.

– Give the victim a fluid that contains electrolytes, such as a commercial sports drink, fruit juice, milk, or ordinary water if that is all that is available. Do not give salt tablets to the victim.

4.3.2. Heat exhaustion. This is a more severe condition than heat cramps and it often affects athletes, fire fighters, construction crews, and factory workers. It can also affect those who wear heavy clothing in a hot and humid environment.

Symptoms of heat exhaustion include cool, moist, pale, ashen, or flushed skin, as well as headache, nausea, dizziness, weakness, and exhaustion. The treatment plan for a victim of this condition is listed below.

– Move the person to a cooler environment with circulating air.

– Remove or loosen as much clothing as possible. Then apply cool, wet, cloths or towels to the skin. Fanning or spraying the person with water can also help.

– If the person is conscious, give them small quantities of a cool liquid, such as a commercial sports drink, fruit juice, or milk to restore their fluids and electrolytes. Water may also be given if that is all that is available. Get them to drink approximately 4 ounces of fluid every 15 minutes.

– If the victim vomits, refuses fluids, if their condition fails to improve, or if they lose consciousness, call 9-1-1 or your local emergency number immediately.

4.3.3. Heat stroke. This is a very serious, potentially fatal condition that usually occurs when the symptoms of heat exhaustion are left untreated. Heat stroke develops when the body's systems are overwhelmed by the heat to the point where they begin to malfunction.

Some symptoms of heat stroke can include: extremely high body temperature, red skin which may be dry or moist, changes in consciousness, rapid or weak pulse, rapid or shallow breathing, confusion, vomiting, and seizures

Heat stroke is life-threatening. Call 9-1-1 or your local emergency number immediately! While waiting for help, you can greatly improve the person's chances of survival by rapidly cooling his or her body.

The best method is to immerse the victim, up to the neck, in a bath of cold water. If this isn't possible, there are alternatives:

– Douse or spray the person with cold water.

– Sponge cool water over the victim's entire body or cover them with towels soaked in iced water. If using towels, rotate these frequently with freshly cooled towels to maintain cooling.

– Cover the victim with bags of ice.

If you are unable to measure and monitor the person's body temperature, apply the above rapid cooling methods for 20 minutes or until the victims' condition improves.

5. Thunderstorms (Hailstorms)

A thunderstorm is considered severe if it produces hail at least one-inch in diameter or has wind gusts of at least 58 miles per hour. The lightning from storms kills more people each year than tornados or hurricanes. The accompanying heavy rain may cause flash flooding, while the high winds can damage homes or blow down trees and utility poles, causing widespread power outages.

Every year, U.S. citizens are needlessly killed or seriously injured by severe storms because they either ignored warnings or failed to hear them. Therefore, it is extremely important to be aware of and understand the following alerts.

Severe Thunderstorm Watch: This means that severe thunderstorms are possible in and near a particular watch area. Stay informed and be ready to act if a warning is issued.

Severe Thunderstorm Warning: This means that severe weather has been reported by spotters or indicated by radar. Warnings indicate imminent danger to life and property.

5.1. How to Prepare

– Learn your local community's emergency warning system for severe thunderstorms.

– Discuss thunderstorm safety with all household members.

– Pick a safe place in your home for everyone to gather during a thunderstorm. This should be away from windows, skylights, and glass doors that could be broken by strong winds, hail, or falling trees.

– Make a list of things to bring inside your house in the event of a severe thunderstorm.

– Keep trees and shrubbery trimmed and free of damaged branches, to improve their wind resistance.

– Protect your pets by ensuring that any outside buildings that house them are as well prepared as your home.

– Consult your local fire department before installing lightning rods.

– Get trained in first aid and learn how to respond to emergencies.

– Maintain an "emergency preparedness kit" (this is covered in the earlier "Bug-Out Bag" chapter).

5.2. HOW TO RESPOND

– Listen to local news or NOAA Weather Radio for updates. Watch for signs of a storm (i.e. darkening skies, lightning flashes, or increasing wind).

– Reschedule outdoor activities if thunderstorms are likely to occur. Many people are struck by lightning even when it is not raining.

– If a severe thunderstorm warning is issued, take shelter in a substantial building or vehicle. Close all windows. Vacate mobile homes that can blow over in high winds.

– If you hear thunder, go indoors immediately! At that point, you're close enough to lightning to be in danger! The National Weather

Service recommends staying indoors for at least 30 minutes after the last audible thunder clap.

– Avoid using telephones or anything else connected to your home's electricity supply. If you have time – unplug everything. Use battery operated equipment instead.

– Shutter windows and close outer doors securely. Keep away from windows.

– Do not take a bath, shower, or use any plumbing.

– If you are driving, safely exit the roadway and park as soon as possible. Do not leave the vehicle. Activate your vehicle's emergency flashers until the heavy rain ends. Avoid touching metal or other surfaces on the vehicle that can conduct electricity.

– If you are outside and away from a secure building, avoid high ground, water, tall, isolated trees, and metal objects (i.e. fences, bleachers, etc.). AVOID picnic shelters, dugouts, and sheds – they are NOT safe.

6. Winter Storms

Winter storms can range from a moderate snowfall over a few hours to blizzards that last for several days. Some are large enough to affect several states, while others target just a single community. Many winter storms are accompanied by dangerously cold temperatures and sometimes by gales, icing, sleet, and freezing rain.

Regardless of their severity, you should prepare for them in order to stay safe. The first step is to learn what the following alert levels mean.

Winter Storm Outlook: Winter storm conditions are possible in the next 2 to 5 days.

Winter Weather Advisory: Weather conditions are expected to cause significant inconveniences and these conditions may be hazardous. Though caution should be exercised, the situation is unlikely to be life threatening.

Winter Storm Watch: Storm conditions are possible within the next 36 to 48 hours. People in a watch area should review their winter storm plans and stay informed on the development of the storm.

Winter Storm Warning: Severe, life threatening, winter conditions are in progress or will begin within the next 24 hours. People in a warning area should take immediate precautions.

6.1. HOW TO PREPARE

– Winterize your vehicle. Keep the gas tank full. (This will also keep the fuel line from freezing.)

– Install storm windows to insulate your home. Alternatively, cover the insides of existing windows with plastic to block out cold air.

– Have heating equipment and chimneys professionally cleaned and inspected every year.

– Before going away during cold weather, leave the heating on in your home and set to a temperature no lower than 55° F.

– Maintain an "emergency preparedness kit" (this is covered in the earlier "Bug-Out Bag" chapter).

6.2. HOW TO RESPOND

– Tune to NOAA Weather or local news channels for critical information from the National Weather Service (NWS).

– Bring pets inside and livestock to sheltered areas. Ensure the animals' access to food and water isn't blocked by snow drifts, ice, etc.

– Run your water faucets, even at a trickle, to prevent pipes freezing.

– All fuel burning equipment should be vented to the outside and kept clear.

– Keep your garage doors closed if water supply lines are in there.

– Open kitchen/bathroom cabinets, allowing warmer air to circulate around plumbing. (Move toxic cleaners and chemicals out of the reach of children!)

– Set your thermostat to the same temperature for both day and night times. This helps avoid bursting pipes.

– Evacuate to a designated public shelter if your home loses power or heat during extremely cold temperatures.

– Avoid driving in sleet, freezing rain, snow, or dense fog. If travel is necessary, keep a disaster supplies kit in your vehicle.

– Before tackling strenuous tasks in cold temperatures, consider your physical condition, the nature of the task, and weather factors.

– Protect yourself from frostbite/hypothermia by wearing warm, loose-fitting, light-weight, clothing in several layers. Stay indoors, if possible.

– Help people who require special assistance, such as elderly people living alone, people with disabilities, and children.

7. Hurricanes

Hurricanes are strong, potentially life threatening, storms that can cause flooding, storm surges, extreme winds, and tornados.

Preparation is the best protection against their dangers. Learn the difference between different hurricane threat levels, as listed below, and then plan accordingly.

Hurricane Watch: Hurricanes may hit within 48 hours. Review your preparations. Be ready to act if warnings are issued. Stay informed.

Hurricane Warning: Hurricanes are expected within 36 hours. Complete your storm preparations. Evacuate the area if instructed to by the authorities.

7.1. HOW TO PREPARE

– Listen to NOAA Weather Radio for critical information.

– Check your disaster supplies. Replace/restock as needed.

– Bring anything indoors that the wind could pick up (bicycles, lawn furniture, etc.).

– Close all windows, doors, and hurricane shutters.

– If you don't have shutters, board up your windows and doors with plywood.

– Turn your refrigerator and freezer to the coldest setting. Keep them closed so the food lasts longer if the power fails.

– Create an evacuation plan and an emergency preparedness kit (as outlined in earlier chapters of this book).

– Find out about your community's hurricane response plan.

Standard homeowner's insurance doesn't cover flooding. It's important to have additional coverage to protect you from damage caused by hurricanes. For more information, please visit the National Flood Insurance Program website at www.FloodSmart.gov.

7.2. How to Respond

Evacuate immediately if you occupy a mobile home, temporary structure, or high-rise building. Evacuation is also necessary if you live on the coast, on a floodplain, near a river, or on an island waterway.

7.2.1. While in Transit

– Follow your evacuation plan (covered earlier in this book).

– Avoid flooded roads and washed out bridges while in transit.

If your home is not in the above categories, stay indoors unless instructed to leave by the local authorities. Follow their orders closely.

7.2.2. While Indoors

– Listen to the radio or TV for information.

– Follow your shelter-in-place plan (covered earlier in this book).

– Turn off propane tanks.

– Avoid using the telephone, except for serious emergencies (there may be risk of electric shock through the phone when lightning strikes).

8. Tornados

Tornados only happen during thunderstorms. They are violently rotating columns of air that extend from the bottom of thunderclouds to the ground. They can demolish buildings, uproot trees, and lethally hurl debris through the air. Tornado intensities are classified on the Fujita Scale with ratings between F0 (weakest) to F5 (strongest). Though more common in the Plains States, tornados can happen anywhere in the U.S.

Tornado Watch: Tornados are possible in and near the watch area. Review and discuss emergency plans. Check your supplies and safe room. Act quickly if a tornado warning is issued or if you suspect one is approaching. Early action saves lives!

Tornado Warning: A tornado has been sighted or detected on radar. There is imminent danger to life and property. Go immediately inside and get to your safe room or underground shelter, if you have either. Be thankful if you have a basement!

8.1. How to Prepare

– During thunderstorms, take note of any mention of tornados as you are listening to the local news or NOAA Weather Radio.

– Know your community's tornado warning system.

– Choose a "safe room" where everyone can gather during a tornado – including your pets. The safest are underground shelters or basements. If these are unavailable, a windowless interior room on the lowest floor of a sturdy building will suffice.

– Practice periodic tornado drills so everyone knows how to respond if one is approaching.

– Consider reinforcing your safe room. Information for this can be found on the FEMA website (http://www.fema.gov).

– Prepare for high winds by removing diseased and damaged limbs from trees.

– Move indoors or secure anything that can be swept up by the wind and become a projectile.

8.1.1. *RECOGNIZE* TORNADO DANGER SIGNS

– Dark, often greenish clouds (caused by hail)

– Wall cloud (an isolated lowering of the base of a thunderstorm)

– Clouds of debris

– Large hailstones

– Funnel clouds (visibly rotating "spout" from the cloud base)

– Roaring noise (that sounds like a freight train)

8.2. HOW TO RESPOND

– Do not wait until you see the tornado!

– Immediately after a tornado warning is issued, gather everyone inside and retreat to your safe room.

– Do not leave your holding room until you are given the all-clear or the thunderstorm has completely subsided.

8.2.1 MOBILE HOMES AND TEMPORARY STRUCTURES

– No matter how sturdy or well tethered they seem, all mobile homes and temporary structures are death traps during a tornado!

– As soon as warnings are received, abandon these properties immediately and hurry to the nearest sturdy building or shelter. Fasten your seat belt if driving.

8.2.2. IF YOU ARE CAUGHT OUTDOORS

– Seek shelter immediately.

– If you cannot quickly walk to shelter, drive to the nearest safe place. Remember to buckle up!

8.2.3. IF YOU ENCOUNTER FLYING DEBRIS WHILE DRIVING

– Immediately pull over and park.

– Stay in the car and keep your seat belt on. Lower your head below the windows, covering it with your hands and a blanket, if possible.

– If you can safely get to a road side ditch, exit your car, lie down in the ditch, and cover your head with your hands.

9. Wildfires

Droughts, dry conditions, and the careless use of fire in heavily wooded areas can all dramatically increase the risk of wildfire. As they often begin unnoticed and spread quickly, speed is critical in combating them! If you live in the country, it is therefore vital to talk to your household about how to deal swiftly with wildfire, as well as how to prevent it from happening in the first place.

9.1. HOW TO PREPARE

– Create an evacuation plan and an emergency preparedness kit (as outlined in earlier chapters of this book).

– Post emergency numbers by every phone in your home.

– Make sure driveway entrances are clearly marked and your house number/address is completely visible.

– Regularly clean roofs and gutters to reduce the amount of flammable debris.

– Select building materials and plants that resist fire.

– Always back your car into the garage or park it in an open space facing the direction of escape.

9.1.1. PREPARING AGAINST SMALL FIRES

You may be forced to fight small outdoor fires before the emergency services arrive. In order to do so:

– Find and maintain an adequate water source outside your house, such as a pond, cistern, well, or swimming pool.

– Set aside household items that can be used as fire tools: a rake, axe, hand or chain saw, bucket, and shovel.

9.2. HOW TO RESPOND

– Be prepared to leave at a moment's notice.

– Listen to local radio and television stations for updated emergency information.

– Put all pets in one room so you can gather them quickly if you need to evacuate.

9.2.1. HOW TO DEAL WITH SMOKE

Wildfire smoke is a killer and is often the biggest danger!

– Limit exposure to smoke and dust.

– Listen and watch for air quality reports and health warnings about smoke.

– Close windows and doors to prevent smoke from getting into the house.

– Use the recycle or recirculate mode on the air conditioner in your home or car. If you don't have this and it is too hot inside with the windows closed, seek shelter elsewhere.

– When smoke levels are high, don't use anything that burns or adds to it, such as candles, fireplaces, or gas stoves. Do not sweep or vacuum – this stirs up the particles that are already inside your home.

– If you have any lung condition, follow medical advice and seek assistance if your symptoms worsen.

10. Tsunamis

Tsunamis are a series of powerful ocean waves generated by severe earthquakes under the seabed. They may also be caused by major landslides into the sea and can strike during the day or night at any time of the year.

When tsunamis enter shallow water, they can rise several feet or, in rare cases, much higher, striking the coast with devastating force.

They may reach land just minutes after an earthquake, engulfing everything and everyone on the beaches and low lying coastal areas.

The tsunami danger period can last for many hours after a major earthquake.

10.1. WHAT IS THE BEST SOURCE OF INFORMATION FOR TSUNAMIS?

10.1.1. The International Tsunami Warning System monitors ocean waves after any Pacific earthquakes with a magnitude greater than 6.5. If these are detected, warnings are issued to local authorities who can order the evacuation of low lying areas if necessary.

10.1.2. The National Oceanic and Atmospheric Administration (NOAA)'s National Weather Service operates two tsunami warning centres:

– West Coast/Alaska Tsunami Warning Center (WC/ATWC), Palmer, Alaska. (Covers Alaska, Washington, Oregon, California, the U.S. Atlantic and Gulf of Mexico coasts, Puerto Rico, the U.S. Virgin Islands, and Canada).

– Pacific Tsunami Warning Centre (PTWC), Ewa Beach, Hawaii. (Serves Hawaii and the U.S. Pacific territories, and serves as an international warning centre for the Pacific and Indian oceans and the Caribbean Sea).

10.2. RECOGNIZING THE SIGNS OF A TSUNAMI

– A strong coastal earthquake that lasts 20 seconds or more.

– A noticeable rapid rise or fall in coastal waters.

10.3. HOW TO PREPARE

– Determine if your home or frequently visited locations are in tsunami hazard areas.

– Plan evacuation routes from each of your frequently visited locations. Try picking areas that are 100 feet above sea level or 2 miles inland from the coast. If this isn't possible, go as high or far away as you can. You should be able to reach your safe location, on foot, within 15 minutes.

– If at-risk, create an evacuation plan and an emergency preparedness kit (as outlined in earlier chapters of this book).

– Know the height of your street above sea level and its distance from the coast or other high-risk waters. Evacuation orders may be based on these.

– Learn the evacuation plans for the public areas you regularly visit that are at-risk from tsunamis.

– If you are a tourist, familiarize yourself with local tsunami evacuation protocols.

10.4. HOW TO RESPOND

10.4.1. If you're on the coast and feel an earthquake that lasts for 20 seconds or longer:

First protect yourself from the earthquake: Drop, cover, and hold on!

When the shaking stops, gather your household members, and immediately move quickly to higher ground away from the coast. A tsunami may be just minutes away!

While on the move, avoid downed power lines.

Avoid buildings and bridges because heavy objects might fall from them during aftershocks.

If on vacation, evacuate to the third floor or above of your hotel if it is a reinforced concrete structure.

10.4.2. If a Tsunami Watch is issued

– Tune to NOAA Weather Radio, the Coast Guard, or local radio/TV stations for emergency updates.

– Locate household members and review evacuation plans. Prepare to move quickly if a warning is issued.

10.4.3. If a Tsunami Warning is issued

– If an official warning is issued or you detect signs of a tsunami, evacuate immediately!

– Grab your emergency preparedness kit and take your pets with you. If it is not safe for you, it's not safe for them either.

– Move to higher ground as far inland as possible.

– Never watch a tsunami! It could put you in mortal danger! If you can see the wave, you are too close to escape it.

Never Put Off Till Tomorrow What You Can Do Today

With hurricanes, tsunamis, acts of terrorism, and even the threat of pandemic influenza filling our headlines and news channels, there has never been such an important time as *now* for having an emergency preparedness plan in place for both you and your loved ones.

Because of this, I hope my book has helped you to address these issues and to become more aware of your surroundings. These tips could save your life whether you are at home, work, or at play.

It is also important to think carefully about the other dangers which could escalate into a disaster. If a major emergency should occur, you must know how to deal with the aftermath effectively.

It is only when you have your plan in place that some of these other possible hazards might come to light. These hazards could have a detrimental effect on your escape or your ability to survive at home – and the last thing you want are any nasty surprises when you were least expecting them!

Having a plan in place will also ensure that everyone in your family will be able to cope with the situation to the best of their ability. Keep in mind that the less stress involved the better and when you are calm you can minimize the risk of using poor judgment. It will also help ensure that everyone will be able to work together effectively as a team.

An important factor of all of this is that careful pre-planning may truly save the lives of any family members who are more vulnerable or who may require special assistance.

The old saying *'Never put off till tomorrow what you can do today,'* has never been truer than when it comes to disaster preparedness.

Because of this, you should always remember that a *prepared* family will always be a *smart* and *safe* family.

About the Author

Judith Turnbridge is a married artist with an interest in interior design. She enjoys painting, calligraphy, and caring for her garden. Her two children have now grown up and flown the nest, and the two hungry mouths she now feeds belong to her two fluffy cats.

Other books by Judith Turnbridge:

Super Simple Home Cleaning: The Best House Cleaning Tips for Green Cleaning the Home

The Super Simple 30-Day Home Cleaning Plan: Making Time to Beat the Grime

How to Organize Your Life to Maximize Your Day: Effective Time Management Tips and Ideas to Simplify Your Life

How to Declutter Your Home for Simple Living: Decluttering Tips and Closet Organization Ideas for Creating Your Own Personal Oasis

Out of Sight, Out of Mind: Easy Home Organization Tips and Storage Solutions for Clutter-Free Living

Nature's Miracle Elixir: The Essential Health Benefits of Coconut Oil